THE KINGFISHER

THE KINGFISHER

Remembering the Magic

JEFF MALDEREZ

A. NOBODY

&

SELF

Jeff Malderez Artist

Contents

bio.site/jeffmalderez

*Elements of AI used, including outline, structure and edits.

First Published 2024. Jeff Malderez, A. Nobody & Self, IngramSpark.

Paperback ISBN: 979-8-9909273-6-0
Hardback ISBN: 979-8-9909273-7-7
Ebook ISBN: 979-8-9909273-8-4

For Charlotte, Amara and Genesis.

Remember the magic, always!

"And above all, watch with glittering eyes the whole world around you because the greatest secrets are always hidden in the most unlikely places. Those who don't believe in magic will never find it."

Roald Dahl

Magic Is That

Magic is that whisper in the wind,
A secret shared by leaves that spin.
It's the sparkle in a child's eye,
The silent wish as stars pass by.

Magic is the dawn's first light,
Chasing shadows, ending night.
It's the dance of fireflies at dusk,
The scent of rain, the earth's sweet musk.

Magic is the bond unseen,
Between hearts where love has been.
It's the dream that fuels the soul,

The unseen thread that makes us whole.

Magic is the artist's brush,
Turning silence into a hush.
It's the song within the breeze,
The gentle sway of ancient trees.

Magic is the border's blur,
Where all are one, no lines deter.
It's the spirit's endless flight,
In the tapestry of night.

Magic is that, and so much more,
A timeless dance on life's vast shore.
It's the essence of the unseen,
The eternal pulse in all that's been.

Magic is that...

Magic is...

Magic.

Prologue

The Forgotten Realm

The realm of Etherea, a place where the veil between the mystical and the mundane is thin, holds a truth known only to those who dare to seek it. Here, the rivers sing of ancient wisdom, the mountains whisper secrets of old, and the winds carry the laughter of the cosmos. It is in this place that Aria, a seeker of truth and artist of visions, finds herself once again on the cusp of a journey. A journey that will take her beyond the known, into the heart of the unknown, where magic and reality intertwine.

Aria, who had once sought the wisdom of the Phoenix and discovered the eternal dance of life, death, and rebirth, now finds herself in a new chapter of her existence. The lessons of the Phoenix have become the foundation of her being, yet a new challenge emerges—a call from the depths of her soul to explore the twelve virtues of existence. These virtues, she senses, are the keys to unlocking a deeper understanding of herself, of humanity, and of the universe.

And so, with a heart full of courage and an artist's spirit, Aria steps into the unknown, where the path of twelve virtues awaits her. Guided by mysterious forces and accompanied by beings of light and wisdom, Aria's journey unfolds in the following chapters, each revealing a truth that transforms her and the world around her. And so, it begins...

1

〜∞〜

Honesty

The Mirror of the Soul

The first light of dawn broke over Etherea, painting the sky with hues of gold and lavender. Aria sat by the edge of a crystalline lake, her sketchbook open on her lap, reflecting the beauty before her. As her fingers moved across the page, capturing the delicate balance of light and shadow, she felt a presence beside her—a flash of iridescent turquoise blue.

It was the Kingfisher, a common bird to most, but not to Aria. To her, this bird was a messenger, a bridge between the world she knew and the deeper mysteries that lay beyond.

"Good morning, Aria," chirped the Kingfisher, his voice both gentle and commanding. "What truth do you seek today?"

Aria smiled, her heart lightened by the bird's presence. "I seek the truth of Honesty, dear friend. How does one see the world and oneself with true eyes?"

The Kingfisher's feathers shimmered as he cocked his head, considering her words. "Honesty is the mirror of the soul, Aria. It is not merely about speaking truth to others but also about seeing yourself without illusion."

With that, the Kingfisher led Aria to the lake's edge, where the water was still and clear. "Look into the water, and what do you see?"

Aria peered into the lake, seeing her reflection staring back at her. But as she gazed deeper, the image began to shift. She saw herself, not as she appeared, but as she truly was—her fears, her desires, her strengths, and her weaknesses, all laid bare.

"It's... overwhelming," she whispered, tears welling in her eyes. "Is this really me?"

The Kingfisher nodded. "Yes, Aria. This is the truth of who you are. Honesty is not about perfection but about acknowledging every part of yourself. Only by accepting your whole self can you begin to grow."

Aria stared at her reflection, the tears now freely falling. It was a humbling experience, to see herself without the filters she had unknowingly placed over her eyes. But as the tears fell, they rippled the surface of the lake, and something incredible happened—the ripples transformed her reflection, blending her image with the world around her. She was no longer just Aria; she was a part of the water, the sky, the earth.

"In truth," the Kingfisher continued, "you are not separate from the world, but a part of it. When you see yourself honestly, you see the connection you share with all things."

With this revelation, Aria felt a profound shift within her. The honesty she sought was not just about facing her own inner truth, but about recognizing her place in the grand tapestry of life. She thanked the Kingfisher, her heart lighter, her vision clearer, and continued on her path, ready to embrace the next virtue.

2

❧

Hope

The Light in the Darkness

As Aria ventured further into Etherea, the landscape began to change. The once bright and open fields gave way to a dense forest, where the canopy above blocked out the sun, casting long shadows on the path ahead. The air was thick with the scent of moss and earth, and the only sound was the distant call of an owl.

In this darkened wood, Aria felt the weight of doubt creeping into her mind. The path was unclear, and every step seemed to lead deeper into the unknown. Her earlier confidence began to wane, and she wondered if she was truly ready to face the challenges ahead.

It was then that Xerxes, the Persian prophet, appeared by her side. His presence was calming, his robes shimmering with a soft light that seemed to push back the darkness.

"Fear not, Aria," Xerxes said, his voice a soothing melody. "This is the forest of doubt, where the light of Hope is born."

Aria looked at him, her eyes wide with confusion. "Hope? But all I see is darkness. How can hope exist here?"

Xerxes smiled, placing a hand on her shoulder. "Hope is not found in the absence of darkness, but within it. It is the light that guides us when all seems lost, the belief that there is a way forward even when the path is hidden."

As he spoke, a small light appeared in the distance—a faint, flickering glow that seemed to dance among the trees. Xerxes gestured towards it. "Follow the light, Aria. Trust in its guidance."

With a deep breath, Aria began to walk towards the light. The darkness around her seemed to grow thicker with each step, but the light remained steady, always just a little ahead. As she moved closer, the shadows began to shift and change, revealing glimpses of the path she had thought lost.

Finally, she reached the source of the light—a single, delicate lantern hanging from the branch of an ancient tree. The lantern's glow was soft but unwavering, a beacon in the night.

"This is the essence of Hope," Xerxes explained, standing beside her. "It is the light that shines in the darkest moments, reminding us that there is always a way forward. It is the belief that even in the face of despair, we can find our way."

Aria reached out to touch the lantern, feeling its warmth. In that moment, she understood. Hope was not a distant dream or a fleeting wish; it was a steady flame within her, a light that would guide her through any darkness.

With renewed strength, Aria thanked Xerxes and continued on her journey, the lantern of Hope now a part of her, lighting her way.

3

Faith

The Bridge to the Unknown

Leaving the forest behind, Aria found herself standing at the edge of a vast chasm. The ground fell away into an abyss so deep that its bottom was lost in shadow. On the other side, she could see the continuation of her path, but there was no bridge, no way across.

As she stared into the depths, a feeling of uncertainty gripped her. How could she possibly cross such a gap? The distance seemed insurmountable, and the void below was terrifying in its emptiness.

It was then that Genesis, the Highly Evolved Being from another realm, appeared before her. Her form was radiant, her presence otherworldly, and her voice echoed with wisdom from beyond the stars.

"Do not be afraid, Aria," Genesis said, her eyes filled with compassion. "This chasm represents the unknown, the great divide between what is and what could be. To cross it, you must have Faith."

Aria looked at her, her heart pounding. "Faith? But how can I have faith when there's no way across?"

Genesis smiled, her gaze unwavering. "Faith is the bridge that connects you to the unknown. It is the trust that, even when you cannot see the path, it exists. Faith is not about knowing what lies ahead, but believing that whatever comes, you have the strength to face it."

With a gentle gesture, Genesis encouraged her to step forward. Aria hesitated, fear gnawing at her resolve. But as she looked into Genesis's eyes, she felt a deep sense of peace. Taking a deep breath, she closed her eyes and took a step into the void.

To her astonishment, she did not fall. Beneath her foot, a bridge of light began to form, extending out into the chasm. Each step she took was met with another segment of the bridge, as if the very act of moving forward created the path itself.

As she crossed, the fear that had once gripped her began to fade, replaced by a profound sense of trust. She did not know what lay ahead, but she no longer needed to. Faith had shown her that the path would reveal itself, one step at a time.

When she reached the other side, Genesis was waiting for her. "You have learned the lesson of Faith, Aria. It is the trust that guides us through the unknown, the belief that we are never alone, even in the darkest moments."

Aria nodded, gratitude swelling in her heart. She had crossed the chasm, not just physically, but spiritually as well. Faith had become a part of her, a guiding force that would carry her through the challenges yet to come.

4

Courage

The Roar of the Heart

The landscape ahead was wild and untamed, with jagged mountains rising high into the sky, their peaks lost in the clouds. The path became steeper, the air thinner, as Aria climbed higher into the mountains of Etherea. The wind howled around her, a fierce and unforgiving force that seemed determined to push her back.

But Aria pressed on, her heart set on the journey. Yet, as she climbed, she began to feel the weight of fear pressing down on her. The heights were dizzying, the drop below perilous. Each step felt like a challenge, and the roar of the wind only amplified the doubts swirling in her mind.

At the summit, she found herself face to face with a great lion, its mane wild and eyes ablaze with a fierce inner fire. The lion's presence was overwhelming, a symbol of raw power and strength.

"You have reached the peak of Courage," the lion growled, its voice echoing through the mountains. "But courage is not the absence of fear; it is the mastery of it."

Aria felt her knees tremble as she faced the lion. "How do I master my fear? It feels so strong, so real."

The lion's eyes softened, and it stepped closer. "Fear is a natural part of the journey, Aria. It is not something to be banished, but something to be understood. Courage is born when you face your fear, acknowledge it, and choose to move forward anyway."

With a deep roar, the lion unleashed a burst of energy that swept over Aria, filling her with a fierce determination. She could feel her fear, but alongside it, she felt something stronger—a fire within her heart, a roar of her own that drowned out the doubts and insecurities.

"This is the roar of the heart," the lion said, its voice now gentle. "It is the voice of Courage, the strength to stand tall in the face of adversity, to move forward even when the path is treacherous."

Aria took a deep breath, feeling the power of Courage within her. She looked out over the mountains, the fear still present but no longer in control. She was the master of her journey, the lion of her own heart.

With a grateful nod to the lion, Aria descended the mountain, her steps sure and strong. Courage was now a part of her, a force that would carry her through the trials ahead.

5

Integrity

The Unbroken Circle

As Aria descended from the mountain, the landscape transformed into a vast plain, where the earth met the sky in an endless horizon. Here, the air was still, and the silence was profound, as if the world itself was holding its breath.

In the center of the plain stood a solitary stone circle, ancient and weathered, yet exuding a powerful energy. As Aria approached, she felt a deep sense of reverence. The stones seemed to hum with a resonance that echoed in her soul.

It was here that Xerxes appeared once again, his form shimmering in the afternoon light. "Welcome to the Circle of Integrity, Aria," he said, his voice filled with wisdom. "This is where you will learn the virtue of living in alignment with your true self."

Aria stepped into the circle, feeling the energy of the stones surround her. "What is Integrity, Xerxes? How does one live with it?"

Xerxes walked to the center of the circle, his gaze steady. "Integrity is the unbroken circle, the state of being whole and undivided. It is living in truth with yourself, aligning your actions with your deepest values and beliefs. When you live with Integrity, your life becomes a reflection of your true self, a mirror of the divine within."

As he spoke, the stones began to glow, each one representing a different aspect of Aria's being—her thoughts, her words, her actions. The glow pulsed in rhythm, creating a harmony that resonated with the beat of her heart.

"To live with Integrity," Xerxes continued, "you must first know yourself, and then choose to live in a way that honors that truth. It is not always easy, for the world will test you, but Integrity is the foundation of a life well-lived."

Aria closed her eyes, feeling the energy of the circle flow through her. She saw moments from her life, times when she had acted in alignment with her true self, and times when she had not. The contrast was stark, and she felt a deep resolve to live with greater Integrity moving forward.

When she opened her eyes, the stones were glowing brightly, their energy now a part of her. She knew that living with Integrity was a daily choice, a commitment to herself and to the divine within her.

With a heart full of determination, Aria stepped out of the circle, the lesson of Integrity now woven into the fabric of her being. She was ready to face whatever lay ahead, knowing that she would do so with truth and honor.

6

Willingness

The Open Door

As Aria continued her journey, the path led her to a great door, tall and imposing, set into a wall of stone. The door was old, its surface covered in intricate carvings that told stories of journeys and quests, of choices made and paths taken.

But the door was closed, and no matter how hard Aria pushed, it would not budge.

It was then that the Kingfisher appeared again, perching on a branch above the door. His feathers glinted in the sunlight, and his eyes sparkled with knowing.

"Aria," the Kingfisher called down, "this door represents the virtue of Willingness. It is not something that can be forced open, but something that must be accepted."

Aria looked up at him, puzzled. "But how do I open it? How do I embrace Willingness?"

The Kingfisher fluttered down to sit on her shoulder, his voice soft in her ear. "Willingness is the open door, the readiness to embrace whatever comes your way. It is about being open to change, to growth, and to the journey itself. The door will open not when you push, but when you are ready to walk through it."

Aria closed her eyes, taking a deep breath. She thought of all the times she had resisted change, clung to the familiar, and feared the unknown. She realized that in order to continue her journey, she needed to let go of that resistance, to be willing to accept whatever lay beyond the door.

With a deep exhale, she let go of her fears and doubts. She felt a shift within her, a softening, an openness. When she opened her eyes, the door was no longer an obstacle but an invitation.

With a gentle push, the door swung open, revealing the path ahead. The Kingfisher chirped in approval, and Aria stepped through, her heart open to whatever lay beyond.

Willingness was now a part of her, a readiness to embrace the unknown with grace and courage. She knew that as long as she remained open, the doors of her journey would continue to open before her.

7

Humility

The Flower in the Dust

The path beyond the door led Aria into a desert, vast and endless, where the sun blazed high in the sky, and the earth cracked beneath her feet. The journey was arduous, the heat intense, and with each step, Aria felt the weight of exhaustion bearing down on her.

As she wandered through the desert, her throat parched and her spirit weary, she came upon a single flower growing in the midst of the barren landscape. It was a simple bloom, small and unassuming, yet its presence in the harsh desert was a miracle in itself.

It was here that Xerxes appeared once more, his form shimmering in the heat. "This is the Flower of Humility, Aria," he said, his voice gentle. "In a place where nothing else grows, it flourishes. Humility is the ability to see the beauty and value in the small, the simple, the overlooked."

Aria knelt beside the flower, marveling at its resilience. "But what does it mean to be humble, Xerxes? How can something so small be so powerful?"

Xerxes smiled, his eyes filled with wisdom. "Humility is not about thinking less of yourself, but about seeing yourself as you truly are—a part of something greater. It is the recognition that we are all equal in the eyes of the universe, that we are all flowers in the desert, each with our own beauty and purpose."

As he spoke, Aria felt a deep sense of peace. She had spent so much of her life striving, reaching for something more, but in this moment, she realized the power of simply being. Of recognizing her place in the world, not as something separate or above, but as a part of the whole.

The flower in the dust became a symbol of this truth. It was small, but it was strong. It did not need to be grand or powerful to have value. It simply was, and that was enough.

With a heart full of humility, Aria rose to her feet. She thanked Xerxes and continued on her journey, the lesson of humility blossoming within her. She knew now that true strength came not from standing above others, but from recognizing the shared humanity in all.

8

~~~~~~~~~

Love

The Heart of the Universe

Aria's journey through the desert eventually led her to an oasis, a place of lush greenery and cool, clear water. It was a place of rest and rejuvenation, a sanctuary in the midst of the harsh desert.

As she drank from the spring and lay beneath the shade of a great tree, she felt a deep sense of peace settle over her. It was here, in this place of serenity, that Genesis appeared once again.

"Aria," Genesis said, her voice filled with warmth, "you have come far on your journey, and now it is time to understand the greatest virtue of all—Love."

Aria looked at her, her heart swelling with emotion. "Love? But I have known love in many forms. What more is there to learn?"

Genesis smiled, her eyes shining with a light that seemed to come from the very heart of the universe. "Love is the essence of all things, the force that binds the universe together. But the love I speak of is not just the love between individuals, but the Love that is the foundation of existence itself."

As she spoke, the oasis around them seemed to come alive. The trees, the water, the very earth pulsed with a gentle energy, a rhythm that Aria could feel deep within her own heart.

"This is the Love that transcends all boundaries," Genesis continued. "It is Love that connects all beings, all things. It is the heartbeat of the universe, the song of creation. It is unconditional, all-encompassing, and eternal."

Aria closed her eyes, letting the energy of the oasis wash over her. She felt the truth of Genesis's words deep in her soul. This was a Love that was not dependent on anything external, a Love that simply was.

It was the love she had always sought, but had never fully understood until now.

When she opened her eyes, Genesis was smiling at her, a look of deep affection in her eyes. "This Love, Aria, is within you, within all of us. It is the essence of who you are. When you live from this place of Love, you are in harmony with the universe, with all that is."

With tears of joy streaming down her face, Aria embraced Genesis, feeling the Love of the universe flow through her. She knew that this was the greatest lesson of all, the one that would guide her for the rest of her days.

Love was not just a feeling, but a state of being, a truth that permeated everything. With this realization, Aria continued on her journey, her heart now the heart of the universe, beating in time with all of creation.

9

Discipline

The Path of the Soul

Leaving the oasis behind, Aria's journey took her into a dense forest, where the path was narrow and winding, with roots and branches constantly threatening to trip her up. The way forward was difficult, requiring focus and determination.

As she navigated the twists and turns of the forest, she began to realize that this part of the journey was not just about physical endurance, but about something deeper—a test of her inner resolve.

It was here that Xerxes appeared once more, his presence a steadying force in the midst of the challenging terrain.

"Aria," Xerxes said, his voice calm and reassuring, "you have learned many virtues on your journey, but now it is time to learn the virtue of Discipline. This path you walk is not just a physical one, but a path of the soul."

Aria paused, catching her breath. "Discipline? But I have faced many challenges. Isn't that enough?"

Xerxes shook his head, his gaze firm. "Discipline is not just about facing challenges; it is about maintaining your commitment to the path, even when it is difficult. It is the practice of aligning your actions with your highest intentions, day after day, moment after moment."

As he spoke, Aria felt a shift within her. She had always been driven by her passions, by her desire to seek the truth, but she realized now that passion alone was not enough. To truly walk the path of the soul, she needed Discipline, the ability to stay the course even when the way was hard, even when her will faltered.

Xerxes gestured to the path ahead, which seemed to stretch on endlessly. "Discipline is the foundation of all growth, Aria. It is what allows you to turn your intentions into reality, to bring your dreams into being. Without it, even the greatest of visions will remain just that—visions."

Aria nodded, understanding now the importance of this virtue. She had come so far, but she knew that the journey was far from over. Discipline would be the key to seeing it through to the end.

With renewed determination, she continued on the path, each step a conscious choice to stay true to her purpose. The forest no longer seemed as daunting, for she knew now that she had the strength within her to navigate it.

Discipline was not about perfection, but about persistence. It was the steady flame that would carry her through the darkest nights, the guiding light that would keep her on the path of the soul.

10

Perseverance

The Mountain of Trials

The forest eventually gave way to a vast mountain range, the peaks towering high above, their summits shrouded in clouds. The air was thin and cold, and the path ahead was steep and treacherous.

Aria stood at the base of the mountain, looking up at the daunting climb before her. The journey so far had tested her in many ways, but she knew that this final ascent would be the greatest challenge yet.

It was here that the Kingfisher appeared once again, his bright plumage a stark contrast to the grey stone of the mountain.

"This is the Mountain of Trials, Aria," the Kingfisher said, his voice filled with both warning and encouragement. "To reach the summit, you must embody the virtue of Perseverance. It is not enough to be strong; you must be steadfast."

Aria nodded, steeling herself for the climb. She began the ascent, the cold biting at her skin, the wind howling in her ears. The path was steep, the rocks loose underfoot, and with every step, she felt the weight of exhaustion pressing down on her.

But Aria did not stop. She kept moving, even when her legs trembled with fatigue, even when her breath came in ragged gasps. She knew that Perseverance was not just about physical endurance, but about the will to keep going, no matter how difficult the journey became.

The higher she climbed, the more the mountain seemed to resist her. The path narrowed, the winds grew stronger, and there were moments when she felt she could not take another step.

But in those moments of doubt, she remembered the lessons she had learned—the Honesty to see her fears, the Hope to light her way, the Faith to trust in the unknown, the Courage to face the trials, the Integrity to stay true to herself, the Willingness to embrace the journey, the Humility to accept her place, the Love that connected her to all, and the Discipline to keep moving forward.

Each virtue became a stepping stone, lifting her higher, carrying her closer to the summit.

Finally, after what felt like an eternity, Aria reached the top. The summit was a small plateau, the sky clear above, the world spread out beneath her in all its glory.

The Kingfisher landed beside her, his eyes filled with pride. "You have learned the lesson of Perseverance, Aria. It is the virtue that carries you through the darkest nights, the longest journeys. It is the strength to keep going, even when the way is hard, even when all seems lost."

Aria looked out over the world, her heart filled with a deep sense of accomplishment. She had faced the trials, she had persevered, and now she stood at the summit, ready to continue her journey.

Perseverance was not just about reaching the end, but about the journey itself, about the strength to keep moving forward, no matter the obstacles.

11

～✦～

Awareness

The Eye of the Soul

From the summit of the mountain, Aria's path led her to a place unlike any she had seen before—a vast expanse of open sky, where the ground seemed to disappear beneath her, leaving her standing on the very edge of the universe.

Here, the stars were close enough to touch, and the air was filled with the soft hum of the cosmos. It was a place of profound silence, where the only sound was the beating of her own heart.

It was in this place that Genesis appeared once more, her form luminous against the backdrop of the universe.

"Welcome to the Realm of Awareness, Aria," Genesis said, her voice resonating with the music of the spheres. "This is where you will learn the final virtue—Awareness, the Eye of the Soul."

Aria looked around in awe, feeling the vastness of the universe within and around her. "What is Awareness, Genesis? How does one attain it?"

Genesis smiled, her eyes filled with infinite wisdom. "Awareness is the ability to see beyond the surface, to perceive the deeper truths of existence. It is the state of being fully present, fully conscious of both yourself and the world around you. It is the recognition that all things are connected, that all is One."

As she spoke, Aria felt a shift in her perception. The stars around her seemed to glow brighter, the hum of the cosmos became clearer, and she could feel the pulse of the universe in her own heart.

"Awareness is not just about seeing with your eyes," Genesis continued, "but about seeing with your soul. It is the ability to perceive the divine in all things, to recognize the unity of all existence."

Aria closed her eyes, letting the energy of the universe flow through her. She felt herself expand, her consciousness merging with the cosmos, until she was no longer just Aria, but a part of the whole—a drop in the ocean of existence.

When she opened her eyes, the world around her had changed. She could see the connections between all things, the threads of light that wove the fabric of the universe together. She could see herself, not as a separate being, but as a part of the grand tapestry of life.

"This is Awareness, Aria," Genesis said, her voice a gentle echo in the vastness. "It is the eye of the soul, the ability to see beyond the illusion of separation, to perceive the truth of oneness. When you live with Awareness, you live in harmony with the universe, in alignment with the divine."

Aria felt a deep sense of peace, a clarity of vision that she had never known before. She thanked Genesis, her heart overflowing with gratitude, and continued her journey, her soul now fully awakened to the truth of existence.

12

Service

The Gift of the Self

With the virtue of Awareness now a part of her, Aria found herself at the final stage of her journey. The path led her to a great temple, a place of light and beauty, where the walls were made of crystal, and the air hummed with the energy of the universe.

As she entered the temple, she was greeted by two groups of cosmic beings—the Wings of Mercury and the Sisterhood of the Sun. These beings of light and wisdom had been guiding her journey from the beginning, though she had not always been aware of their presence.

"Welcome, Aria," the leader of the Wings of Mercury said, his voice like the chiming of bells. "You have learned the virtues, and now it is time to learn the final lesson—Service."

Aria looked at them, her heart filled with a deep sense of purpose. "What is Service? How can I serve?"

The leader of the Sisterhood of the Sun stepped forward, her presence warm and nurturing. "Service is the gift of the Self, Aria. It is the act of giving of yourself to others, to the world, to the universe. It is the recognition that your journey is not just for you, but for all beings. When you serve, you become a vessel of the divine, a channel through which the light of the universe flows."

As she spoke, Aria felt a deep sense of connection to all that was around her. She understood now that her journey had been not just about her own growth, but about preparing her to serve others, to share the wisdom she had gained, to be a light in the world.

The temple around her seemed to glow brighter, and Aria felt the presence of the Self, the divine Magician, the source of all things. She understood now that Service was not just an act, but a state of being, a way of living in harmony with the universe, in alignment with the divine.

With a heart full of love and a soul full of light, Aria stepped forward, ready to embrace her new role. She knew now that her journey was just beginning, that the path of Service would lead her to places she could not yet imagine, but she was ready.

For she had learned the greatest truth of all—that we are all One, that the universe is a grand tapestry of love and light, and that the greatest joy comes from serving that light, from being a part of the dance of creation.

And so, Aria set out on her new journey, the Kingfisher by her side, Xerxes guiding her steps, Genesis lighting her way, and the Wings of Mercury and the Sisterhood of the Sun watching over her.

For she was now a servant of the universe, a beacon of light, a vessel of the divine.

And the magic of the Kingfisher, the Phoenix, and the Self lived on, in her and in all beings, forever and always, in the eternal dance of life, death, and rebirth.

Epilogue

The Unity of All

In the end, Aria's journey was not just her own, but a reflection of the journey that all beings take. It was a reminder that we are all connected, that we are all One, and that the virtues of Honesty, Hope, Faith, Courage, Integrity, Willingness, Humility, Love, Discipline, Perseverance, Awareness, and Service are the keys to living in harmony with the universe.

For in the grand tapestry of existence, we are all threads, woven together in a pattern of infinite beauty and complexity. Each of us has a role to play, a light to shine, a truth to share and a gift - a medicine - to give to aid others on their path.

And as we walk our own paths, we are never alone, for the Kingfisher, the Phoenix, the Self, and all the beings of light and wisdom are with us, guiding us, teaching us, loving us.

In the end, dear reader, remember this: You are a part of the universe, a thread in the grand tapestry of existence. Embrace your journey with love, with light, and with the knowledge that you are never alone.

For we are all One, eternally connected, infinitely divine.

And the magic of the Kingfisher lives within you, forever and always...

...It's inside you.

The last place you'll ever likely look.

But there it is.

There's the magic of life waiting to be remembered.

Waiting for it to be realized.

It's waiting to be embodied eternally ...as YOU!

"Once more...just like before."

Said the Kingfisher...

"Remember the magic!"

Appendix I

Messages from The Wings of Mercury

Embrace Your Inner Light:

The Wings of Mercury, messengers of the Self, teach that each being carries a spark of divine light within. This light is not just a guide through darkness but a beacon that can illuminate the path for others. By embracing your inner light, you align with your true purpose, allowing your actions to reflect the divine love and wisdom that flows through you. It is this light that connects you to the greater cosmic harmony, reminding you that your existence is both unique and interconnected with all that is.

Trust in the Divine Flow:

The Wings of Mercury emphasize the importance of trusting in the divine flow of life. They remind us that the universe operates in perfect harmony, even when we cannot see the larger picture. By surrendering to this flow, you open yourself to the infinite possibilities that the universe has in store for you. Trusting in this flow means letting go of fear and resistance, allowing the universe to guide you towards your highest good with grace and ease.

Serve with Compassion and Humility:

The Wings of Mercury encourage all beings to serve others with compassion and humility. Service is not about seeking recognition or reward but about selflessly offering your talents and love for the betterment of all. By serving with an open heart, you become a channel for the divine, spreading peace, love, and healing throughout the universe. This act of service is a powerful expression of unity, reminding us that we are all one, and that through service, we contribute to the collective upliftment of all beings.

On Time:

Infinity is not measured or counted within the spectrum of time. It's beyond the illusion of a linear progression and sequence of events. Rather it is; simply, wholly, completely, and eternally.

In the spotlight (of awareness):

Remember that co-creation with that which is infinite is a great joy for the soul. Paradox and mystery combine to produce doorways within the Self. More is being revealed as She walks through Her own blissful forgetting. Mystical waters drift by the prophetic unknown in ripples of Self-awareness. A journey with no end, we find meaning and purpose within the One who is laughing with us all. All that ever was, is and ever will be, finds existence now. Beautiful regrets release tears from fears and awe for those who vibe with mind and heart together, divinely connected. Twelve inches between the two, awareness of a bridge for connection in unity. Here's your present...

Appendix II

The Sisterhood of the Sun whisper

E Pluribus Unum:

When will we be true to the words: "E Pluribus Unum", in thought, action, and being? For there are no walls in heaven, nor borders in Valhalla, no separation in Satori, or restrictions in Jannah. For we are One with all, and the One is all infinitely. Just like love divinely expressed within every heart of ours. Know thy Self and to thine own Self be true, now and always. For united we stand, lest we fall...divided – separated by illusions of 'us and them'.

The Child Within:

A return to the child within, not in codependency, but with wonder and in awe of the beauty of life and the firm belief in the magic of creation Herself. And that we are a part of that at core. The child within knows this and witnesses the new with a purity of innocence, and of a joy, that rivals the magnitude of bliss contained within the brightest of angels' smiles.

Honor the Earth as Sacred:

The Sisters of the Sun teach that the Earth is a living, breathing entity deserving of reverence and care. They remind us that all life is interconnected, and that by honoring the Earth, we honor ourselves and future generations. Every tree, river, mountain, and creature is part of a delicate balance that sustains life. By treating the Earth as sacred, we align ourselves with the natural rhythms of the universe, fostering a deep respect and love for all living beings.

Live in Harmony with Nature:

The Sisters of the Sun emphasize the importance of living in harmony with nature, recognizing that humanity's well-being is intrinsically tied to the health of the planet. They encourage us to live sustainably, to be mindful of our consumption, and to protect the natural world from harm. By living in harmony with nature, we contribute to the healing of the Earth, ensuring that its beauty and abundance can be enjoyed by all creatures for generations to come.

Nurture the Light Within All Beings:

The Sisters of the Sun advocate for nurturing the light within all beings, recognizing the divine presence in every soul. They teach that love, compassion, and kindness are the most powerful forces in the universe, capable of transforming even the darkest of circumstances. By nurturing the light within others—whether through acts of kindness, support, or simply by recognizing their inherent worth—we create a ripple effect of positivity and healing that spreads throughout the world, contributing to the collective evolution of humanity and the Earth.

Appendix III

Transmissions from Genesis

The Unity of All Beings:

Genesis teaches that humility begins with the understanding that all beings, regardless of their form or origin, are expressions of the same divine essence. In her realm of existence, there is no hierarchy, only the recognition of the intrinsic value in every soul. By embracing this truth, we learn to approach others with reverence and compassion, seeing them as reflections of the same light that resides within us.

The Dance of Interconnectedness:

In Genesis's realm, all of existence is viewed as a vast, interconnected dance of energy and consciousness. She imparts that humility comes from recognizing our role in this dance—not as the center, but as one of many vital participants. This understanding fosters a sense of respect for the contributions of all beings, teaching us to move through life with grace, aware of the delicate balance that sustains the cosmos.

The Power of Surrender:

Genesis shares that in her realm, true wisdom is found not in control, but in the power of surrender. Humility is the ability to let go of the need to dominate or dictate the flow of life, trusting instead in the divine intelligence that orchestrates the universe. By surrendering our egoic desires, we open ourselves to the boundless wisdom and love that permeates all of existence.

The Realm Beyond Time and Space:

Genesis's existence transcends the limitations of time and space, offering a perspective of reality where all moments and places converge in a singular now. She teaches that humility involves stepping beyond our limited perceptions and embracing the vastness of the universe. This expanded awareness allows us to see our lives as part of a much larger tapestry, fostering a deep sense of humility in the face of the infinite.

The Wisdom of Silence:

Genesis emphasizes that in her realm, silence is a profound source of wisdom. Humility is not only found in words and actions but in the ability to listen deeply—to the universe, to others, and to our inner selves. In the silence, we connect with the universal wisdom that transcends language, learning to appreciate the mysteries that cannot be spoken, only felt. This silence nurtures humility, reminding us that the most profound truths often lie beyond the reach of words.

www.ingramcontent.com/pod-product-compliance
Lightning Source LLC
Chambersburg PA
CBHW040848120626
46547CB00001B/77